Czech Re

A
Pocket Travel
Guide 2023

EXPLORE THE BEST OF CZECH REPUBLIC
RICH HISTORY, TOP ATTRACTIONS, GEMS
WITH THIS COMPREHENSIVE GUIDE

DANIEL C. FLICK

TABLE OF CONTENT

2. U KROKA
3. KRČMA
4. HOSPŮDKA U KMOTRA
5. RESTAURACE MLEJNICE

TOP FIVE BARS STATIONS

U SUDU - PRAGUE

VINÁRNA U KŘÍŽŮ - BRNO

PIVOVAR U TŘÍ RŮŽÍ - PRAGUE

LOKÁL - PRAGUE

U FLEKŮ - PRAGUE

TOP FIVE NIGHTLIFE PLACES

ROXY - PRAGUE

CROSS CLUB - PRAGUE

LUCERNA MUSIC BAR - PRAGUE

MUSIC CLUB MALÝ GLEN - BRNO

MECCA CLUB - PRAGUE

CHAPTER EIGHT: PRACTICAL INFORMATION

MONEY MATTERS

HEALTH AND SAFETY

USEFUL CONTACT INFORMATION IN THE CZECH REPUBLIC

FINAL TIPS AND RECOMMENDATIONS FOR YOUR TRIP TO THE CZECH REPUBLIC:

FAREWELL TO CZECH

Czech Map

WELCOME TO CZECH REPUBLIC

Once upon a time, nestled in the heart of Central Europe, there lay a land of enchantment known as the Czech Republic. Its story begins with a rich tapestry of history, woven through the centuries, and it beckons us to embark on a remarkable journey through time.

Picture yourself transported to a bygone era, where fairytale castles dot the lush green landscapes, and cobblestone streets wind their way through charming medieval towns. As you step foot in this magical land, you can almost hear the whispers of the past echoing through the air, telling tales of kings and queens, knights and princesses.

One of the first chapters of this captivating tale unfolds in the ancient city of Prague, the crown jewel of the Czech Republic. Gaze in awe at the majestic Prague Castle, perched high atop a hill, overlooking the city with its Gothic spires and Renaissance facades. Lose yourself in the labyrinthine streets of the Old Town, where every corner reveals a hidden gem - from the astronomical marvel of the Prague Orloj, the oldest working astronomical clock in the world, to the haunting beauty of the Charles Bridge, adorned with statues of saints and guarded by the mighty Vltava River.

But the Czech Republic's allure extends far beyond its capital. Venture into the picturesque countryside and discover a land untouched by time. Wander through the fairytale town of Český Krumlov, where a meandering river wraps around a medieval castle, creating a scene straight out of a storybook. Explore the captivating landscapes of Bohemian Switzerland National Park, where soaring sandstone cliffs and lush forests transport you to a world of natural wonders.

Immerse yourself in the cultural tapestry of the Czech Republic, where the arts have flourished for centuries. Be enchanted by the haunting melodies of Bedřich Smetana's "The Moldau," an orchestral piece that captures the essence of the country's beloved river. Lose yourself in the captivating works of art by Alfons Mucha, the renowned Art Nouveau painter. And of course, indulge in the rich flavors of Czech cuisine, from hearty goulash and tender roasted pork knuckle to the world-famous Pilsner beer, brewed with passion and precision.

As you delve deeper into this storybook land, you'll uncover a nation that cherishes its traditions and embraces its heritage. From colorful folk festivals and lively village celebrations to the joyous ringing of Christmas markets, the Czech Republic invites you to become a part of its vibrant tapestry of life.

So, dear traveler, with a twinkle in your eye and a sense of wonder in your heart, welcome to the Czech Republic. Let the pages of this extraordinary story unfold before you, as you discover a land where history, beauty, and enchantment intertwine in the most magical of ways.

TOP TEN REASONS TO VISIT CZECH REPUBLIC

Rich History

The Czech Republic is a treasure trove of history, with roots dating back to the Middle Ages. From the grandeur of Prague Castle, the largest ancient castle complex in the world, to the intricate details of the Astronomical Clock in Prague's Old Town Square, history comes alive in every corner. Walk across the iconic Charles Bridge, lined with statues and offering breathtaking views of the Vltava River, and you'll feel transported to another era.

Prague's Architectural Beauty

Prague is renowned for its stunning architecture, a harmonious blend of Gothic, Renaissance, Baroque, and Art Nouveau styles. Admire the Gothic masterpiece of St. Vitus Cathedral, which took centuries to complete, and explore the elegant Prague Castle complex. Marvel at the whimsical Art Nouveau facades, such as the Municipal House and the iconic Dancing House. Prague's architectural splendor is a feast for the eyes.

Fairytale Towns

Beyond Prague, the Czech Republic boasts a collection of fairytale towns that seem straight out of storybooks. Český Krumlov, a UNESCO World Heritage site, enchants visitors with its medieval castle, winding streets, and the Vltava River meandering through its center. Telč captivates with its colorful Renaissance-style houses surrounding a picturesque square, while Kutná Hora intrigues with its haunting Bone Church, adorned with human bones.

Castles and Chateaux

The Czech Republic is home to an impressive array of castles and chateaux, each with its own unique charm. Explore Karlštejn Castle, perched on a hilltop and guarding the Czech crown jewels, or immerse yourself in the romantic atmosphere of Hluboká Castle, resembling a fairytale palace. Other notable castles include Konopiště Castle, once home to Archduke Franz Ferdinand, and Český Šternberk Castle, offering panoramic views of the surrounding countryside.

Natural Beauty

Nature lovers will find solace in the Czech Republic's breathtaking landscapes. Bohemian Switzerland National Park, located on the border with Germany, features dramatic sandstone formations, deep gorges, and enchanting hiking trails. Moravian Karst reveals a mysterious underground world of caves and caverns waiting to be explored. Šumava National Park offers serene forests, glacial lakes, and opportunities for hiking, biking, and wildlife spotting.

Spa Towns and Hot Springs

The Czech Republic has a long-standing tradition of spa culture, where visitors can indulge in relaxation and rejuvenation. Karlovy Vary, with its elegant colonnades and healing thermal springs, has been a favorite retreat for centuries. Mariánské Lázně entices with its Belle Époque charm and beautiful parks. Discover the healing properties of the country's mineral-rich waters and pamper yourself with spa treatments and wellness therapies.

Czech Beer and Brewing Tradition

The Czech Republic is a beer lover's paradise. It is famous for its exceptional brewing heritage and boasts the highest beer consumption per capita in the world. Visit local breweries, such as Pilsner Urquell or Budweiser Budvar, and learn about the art of brewing Czech lagers and Pilsners. Enjoy a pint in traditional beer halls, where lively conversations flow and Czech hospitality shines.

Bohemian Glass

The Czech Republic has a long-standing reputation for producing exquisite glassware. Discover the art of glassmaking in famous glassworks like Moser or Rückl, where skilled craftsmen shape molten glass into stunning pieces of art. From delicate crystal stemware to colorful glass sculptures, Bohemian glass is admired worldwide for its brilliance and craftsmanship.

Cultural Festivals

The Czech Republic celebrates its rich cultural heritage through a vibrant calendar of festivals. The Prague Spring International Music Festival brings world-class musicians to the city, offering classical concerts and opera performances. The Karlovy Vary International Film Festival attracts filmmakers and cinephiles from around the globe. Experience the festive atmosphere of Easter markets or the magical charm of Christmas markets, where traditional crafts, mulled wine, and festive treats await.

Warm Hospitality and Local Cuisine

The Czech people are known for their warm and welcoming nature, ensuring visitors feel at home. Engage with the locals, learn about their traditions, and immerse yourself in the cultural fabric of the country. Indulge in Czech cuisine, which is hearty, flavorful, and often accompanied by the country's renowned beer. Try traditional dishes like svíčková (marinated beef with creamy sauce), goulash, or vepřo-knedlo-zelo (roasted pork with dumplings and sauerkraut) for a true taste of Czech gastronomy.

In the Czech Republic, history, culture, natural beauty, and warm hospitality blend seamlessly, creating a captivating destination that leaves a lasting impression on every visitor. Prepare to be enthralled by its rich tapestry of experiences and discover why this land nestled in Central Europe holds a special place in the hearts of those who venture here.

CHAPTER ONE ABOUT CZECH REPUBLIC

History of Czech Republic

The history of the Czech Republic is a tale of resilience, cultural flourishing, and political transformations. The roots of Czech history can be traced back to the early Slavic tribes that settled in the region. Over the centuries, the Czech lands were shaped by various ruling powers, dynasties, and empires.

In the 9th century, the Great Moravian Empire emerged, establishing the foundations of the Czech statehood. However, in the 10th century, the Bohemian princes took control and established the Přemyslid dynasty, which would shape the destiny of the Czech lands for centuries to come.

Under the rule of the Přemyslids, the Czech lands experienced a period of prosperity, with Prague emerging as a significant center of trade and culture. The 14th century witnessed the reign of King Charles IV, who transformed Prague into a magnificent capital and established the first university in Central Europe, the Charles University.

In the 15th century, the Hussite movement, led by Jan Hus, challenged the authority of the Catholic Church. The Hussites fought for religious and social reforms, igniting a series of religious conflicts known as the Hussite Wars. These conflicts marked a turning point in Czech history and contributed to the emergence of a strong Czech national consciousness.

The 16th and 17th centuries were marked by the rule of the Habsburg dynasty, which brought the Czech lands under the control of the Holy Roman Empire. During this period, the Czech lands experienced religious tensions as the Protestant Reformation spread throughout Europe.

In the 19th century, Czech nationalism gained momentum, advocating for cultural and political autonomy within the multinational Austro-Hungarian Empire. The Czech National Revival, led by prominent figures such as František Palacký and

Jan Neruda, aimed to revive Czech language, literature, and cultural heritage.

The end of World War I brought significant changes to the region. In 1918, Czechoslovakia, a new democratic state, was founded, encompassing Czech and Slovak territories. Tomáš Garrigue Masaryk became the first president, and the country thrived, embracing modernization and democracy.

However, the peaceful coexistence of Czechs and Slovaks faced challenges in the interwar period, and tensions arose. In 1938, the Munich Agreement led to the dismemberment of Czechoslovakia, with Nazi Germany occupying the Czech lands, and Slovakia becoming a separate state.

World War II brought great suffering to the Czech lands as they fell under German occupation. Resistance movements emerged, and the assassination of Nazi official Reinhard Heydrich in 1942 by Czechoslovak paratroopers became a symbol of Czech resistance.

With the end of World War II, Czechoslovakia was restored and entered a period of communist rule under Soviet influence. The communist era lasted until the Velvet Revolution in 1989 when a peaceful popular uprising led by Václav Havel and other dissidents brought an end to communist rule.

In 1993, Czechoslovakia peacefully split into two separate countries, the Czech Republic and Slovakia. The Czech Republic continued its path toward democracy, joining the European Union in 2004 and becoming an important player in Central European politics and economy.

Today, the Czech Republic stands as a thriving nation, known for its rich cultural heritage, architectural splendors, and a vibrant democracy. The country continues to evolve, embracing its history while embracing modernity and welcoming visitors from around the world to experience its captivating past and promising future.

Cultures of Czech

The Czech Republic is a country with a diverse and vibrant cultural scene, shaped by its rich history, traditions, and the fusion of various influences. Czech culture encompasses literature, music, art, architecture, cuisine, and a strong sense of national identity. Here are some key aspects of Czech culture:

Literature: Czech literature has a long and illustrious history. The works of renowned authors like Franz Kafka, Milan Kundera, Bohumil Hrabal, and Karel Čapek have achieved international recognition. The Czech Republic also takes pride in its fairy tales and folklore, with famous tales such as those collected by Karel Jaromír Erben and Božena Němcová.

Music: Music holds a special place in Czech culture. The country has produced many celebrated composers, including Antonín Dvořák, Bedřich Smetana, and Leoš Janáček. Prague is a hub for classical music, hosting the prestigious Prague

Spring International Music Festival, where renowned orchestras and musicians gather to perform. Folk music, with its distinctive melodies and lively dances, is also an integral part of Czech culture.

Art and Architecture: The Czech Republic boasts a wealth of artistic and architectural treasures. The Art Nouveau movement left an indelible mark on Czech architecture, with notable works by Alfons Mucha and the unique designs of the Prague Municipal House. The country's medieval and Renaissance architecture is showcased in its castles, chateaux, and historic towns. Prague's art scene flourishes with galleries, museums, and contemporary art exhibitions.

Cuisine: Czech cuisine is known for its hearty and flavorsome dishes. Traditional Czech meals often feature meat, potatoes, and cabbage. Iconic dishes include svíčková (marinated beef with creamy sauce), vepřo-knedlo-zelo (roasted pork with dumplings and sauerkraut), and trdelník (sweet pastry roll). The Czech Republic is also famous for its beer culture, with a long brewing tradition and renowned brands like Pilsner Urquell and Budweiser Budvar.

Festivals and Traditions: The Czech Republic celebrates its cultural heritage through numerous festivals and traditions. The Easter markets and Christmas markets, held in cities and towns across the country, offer a magical atmosphere with crafts, food, and traditional performances. The Masopust carnival, with its colorful parades and costumes, heralds the arrival of spring. Folk festivals showcase traditional music, dances, and costumes, allowing visitors to immerse themselves in Czech folklore.

Sports: Czechs have a strong passion for sports, with ice hockey, football (soccer), and tennis being particularly popular. The Czech Republic has produced many successful athletes, including hockey legends Jaromír Jágr and Dominik Hašek, tennis stars like Martina Navratilova and Petra

Kvitová, and footballers such as Pavel Nedvěd and Tomáš Rosický.

National Identity: The Czech Republic has a strong sense of national identity and pride, forged through its history of resilience, cultural achievements, and the struggle for independence. Czechs value their language, customs, and traditions, and take pride in their contributions to literature, music, and science.

Czech culture is a tapestry woven from centuries of history, artistic endeavors, and a deep appreciation for traditions. Whether exploring Prague's architectural gems, attending a classical music concert, or savoring traditional cuisine, visitors to the Czech Republic are sure to be immersed in a vibrant and captivating cultural experience.

Geography and climate change of Czech Republic

The Czech Republic, located in the heart of Central Europe, boasts a diverse and picturesque geography. The country is landlocked and bordered by Germany to the west, Austria to the south,

Slovakia to the east, and Poland to the northeast. Let's explore its geography and the impacts of climate change on the Czech Republic.

Geographically, the Czech Republic can be divided into three main regions: Bohemia, Moravia, and Silesia. Bohemia, in the west, is characterized by rolling plains, river valleys, and picturesque landscapes. Moravia, in the east, is known for its fertile lowlands, vineyards, and wine production. Silesia, located in the northeast, encompasses the mountainous areas of the country.

The country's most prominent geographic feature is the Bohemian Massif, which includes the Sudetes Mountains in the north and the Šumava Mountains in the southwest. The highest peak in the Czech Republic is Sněžka, standing at 1,603 meters (5,259 feet) in the Krkonoše (Giant Mountains). Other notable mountain ranges include the Jeseníky Mountains and the Beskids.

The Czech Republic is also known for its numerous rivers. The Vltava River, flowing through Prague, is the longest river entirely within the country. Other significant rivers include the Elbe (Labe), Morava, and Oder (Odra), which form part of the country's natural borders.

As for climate change, the Czech Republic, like many regions across the globe, is experiencing its effects. Rising global temperatures and changing weather patterns have led to various impacts on the country's environment. Some key aspects of climate change in the Czech Republic include:

Temperature Increase: The average temperatures in the Czech Republic have been rising. Winters have become milder, with reduced snowfall in some areas. Summers have seen more heatwaves, leading to increased demand for cooling and potential risks to human health.

Precipitation Changes: The patterns of precipitation have been altered, resulting in more intense rainfall events and the potential for floods. Heavy downpours can lead to flash floods, affecting river systems and infrastructure. Conversely, some regions may experience periods of drought, affecting agriculture and water resources.

Ecosystem Shifts: Climate change can impact the country's ecosystems, with potential changes in the distribution of plant and animal species. Warmer temperatures may affect the growth patterns of forests, while shifts in precipitation patterns may impact wetland habitats.

Water Resources: Changes in precipitation patterns and the availability of water sources can affect water resources in the country. Droughts can lead to decreased water availability for agricultural, industrial, and domestic use, while heavy rainfall events can strain water management systems.

The Czech Republic acknowledges the importance of addressing climate change and has implemented measures to mitigate its impacts. The country has set renewable energy targets, invested in sustainable infrastructure, and participated in international climate agreements.

Through these efforts, the Czech Republic aims to reduce greenhouse gas emissions, adapt to changing climatic conditions, and promote sustainable practices to protect its environment and ensure a prosperous future.

While the impacts of climate change pose challenges, the Czech Republic remains committed to environmental stewardship, sustainable development, and finding innovative solutions to mitigate and adapt to the changing climate.

CHAPTER TWO: PLANNING YOUR TRIP

Budgeting for Czech Republic

When planning a budget for a trip to the Czech Republic, it's essential to consider various expenses such as accommodation, transportation, meals, activities, and miscellaneous costs. Here's a brief overview of how you can allocate your budget:

- Accommodation: The cost of accommodation in the Czech Republic can vary depending on the city and type of lodging. In Prague, for example, you can find a range of options from budget-friendly hostels to luxury hotels. On average, budget around $30 to $100 per night for a decent hotel or hostel, although prices can fluctuate depending on the season.

- Transportation: Public transportation in the Czech Republic is efficient and affordable. For getting around within cities, consider using trams, buses, or the metro, with ticket prices ranging from $1 to $2 per journey. If you plan to travel between cities, trains and buses are convenient options, with ticket prices varying based on the distance. Allocate around $10 to $30 for intercity transportation.

- Meals: Czech cuisine offers a range of affordable dining options. In local restaurants or pubs, a traditional Czech meal can cost around $8 to $15 per person. If you prefer self-catering, you can find groceries at reasonable prices. Additionally, street food stalls and bakeries offer affordable and tasty options. Budget around $20 to $30 per day for meals, but this can vary depending on your preferences.

- Activities: The Czech Republic offers a wealth of cultural, historical, and outdoor activities. Admission fees for attractions like Prague Castle, museums, and galleries can range from $5 to $15 per person. Budget extra for any guided tours or special experiences you might want to participate in. Outdoor activities such as hiking or exploring national parks are often free or have minimal costs. Allocate around $50 to $100 for activities and attractions, depending on your interests.

- Miscellaneous Costs: It's important to allocate some funds for miscellaneous expenses like souvenirs, snacks, drinks, and incidentals. Budget around $10 to $20 per day for these additional expenses.

Remember to consider currency exchange rates and any fees associated with money conversion or ATM withdrawals when planning your budget. It's also wise to have a contingency fund for unforeseen expenses or emergencies.

Overall, the daily budget for a trip to the Czech Republic can range from around $60 to $150 per person, depending on your preferences, comfort level, and the duration of your stay. With careful planning and consideration, you can enjoy a wonderful experience in the Czech Republic without breaking the bank.

When to visit

The Czech Republic is a year-round destination, each season offering its own unique charm and activities. The optimum time to visit is determined by your interests and the kind of experiences you desire. To help you determine when to schedule your vacation, here's a summary of the seasons:

Spring (April to June): Spring is a beautiful time to visit the Czech Republic as the weather gradually warms up, and nature comes alive. April and May tend to be quieter, with fewer crowds and moderate temperatures. June marks the beginning of summer, with longer days and pleasant weather for exploring cities and outdoor activities. Spring is ideal for those who prefer milder temperatures and wish to avoid the peak tourist season.

Summer (July to August): Summer is the peak tourist season in the Czech Republic, especially in popular destinations like Prague. The weather is generally warm, with average temperatures ranging from 20°C to 25°C (68°F to 77°F). It's a great time to enjoy outdoor festivals, visit castles, explore national parks, and indulge in outdoor dining. However, expect greater crowds and increased lodging expenses around this time.

Autumn (September to October): Autumn in the Czech Republic offers mild temperatures, stunning foliage, and fewer tourists compared to summer. September is particularly pleasant, with comfortable weather for exploring cities and outdoor activities. October can be slightly cooler, but it's a fantastic time to witness the vibrant colors of autumn foliage. Autumn is ideal for those seeking a quieter travel experience and appreciating the natural beauty of the Czech landscapes.

Winter (November to February): Winter brings a magical atmosphere to the Czech Republic, especially during the holiday season. December is particularly festive, with Christmas markets adorning the cities. If you don't mind colder temperatures, winter is a great time to visit if you're interested in winter sports, such as skiing and snowboarding in the mountainous regions. Prague, in particular, offers a charming ambiance with fewer crowds. Simply prepare for colder weather and fewer daylight hours.

the best time to visit

Considering the overall weather and crowd conditions, the best times to visit the Czech Republic are during the shoulder seasons of spring (April to June) and autumn (September to October). These periods offer pleasant weather, fewer crowds, and the opportunity to enjoy outdoor activities comfortably. However, each season has its own allure, so choose based on your preferences and the experiences you desire.

Ultimately, regardless of the time you visit, the Czech Republic has something to offer year-round, be it historical sites, cultural festivals, natural beauty, or the warmth of Czech hospitality.

Visa to Czech Republic

The Czech Republic visa requirements vary based on your nationality, as well as the purpose and length of your travel. Here is a general overview of the visa process for visiting the Czech Republic:

- Schengen Visa: The Czech Republic is a member of the Schengen Area, which allows for the free movement of individuals across its member countries. If you are a citizen of a country that is not exempt from visa requirements, you will need to apply for a Schengen Visa.

- Visa Exemptions: Citizens of certain countries, such as the United States, Canada, Australia, and many European countries, are exempt from the Schengen Visa requirement and can enter the Czech Republic for up to 90 days in a 180-day period for tourism or business. However, it's important to check the latest visa requirements and exemptions based on your nationality and purpose of visit.

- Types of Visas: If you plan to stay in the Czech Republic for more than 90 days or have a specific purpose such as work, study, or family reunification, you will need a long-term visa or residency permit. These visas have specific requirements and must be obtained before traveling to the Czech Republic.

Visa Application Process: To apply for a visa, you will typically need to submit the following documents:

1. A completed visa application form.
2. A valid passport with at least six months' validity beyond your planned stay.
3. Two recent passport-sized photographs.
4. Proof of comprehensive travel medical insurance that covers you for the length of your visit.
5. Proof of accommodation arrangements in the Czech Republic.
6. Proof of enough financial resources to maintain oneself throughout your stay.

7. Flight itinerary or travel reservations.

Additional documents may be required depending on the purpose of your visit (e.g., invitation letter, employment contract, student enrollment letter, etc.).

- Visa Application Submission: Visa applications are usually submitted at the Czech embassy or consulate in your home country or the country where you have legal residence. It's advisable to make an appointment in advance and ensure that you have all the required documents and fees ready.
- Visa Processing Time: The visa processing time can vary, so it's recommended to apply well in advance of your planned travel dates. Processing times can range from a few days to several weeks, depending on the embassy or consulate and the complexity of your application.

It's important to note that visa requirements and procedures can change, so it's advisable to consult the official website of the Czech embassy or consulate in your country or seek guidance from the nearest diplomatic mission to get the most up-to-date information regarding visa requirements.

Always ensure that you have a valid visa or exemption before traveling to the Czech Republic to avoid any travel disruptions or issues at the border.

Entry requirement

Entry requirements for the Czech Republic vary depending on your nationality and the purpose and duration of your visit. Here is a general overview of the entry requirements for visiting the Czech Republic:

- Passport: All visitors must possess a valid passport to enter the Czech Republic. Check that your passport is valid for at least six months beyond the duration of your intended stay.
- Visa Requirements: Citizens of certain countries are exempt from visa requirements

and can enter the Czech Republic for tourism or business purposes for up to 90 days within a 180-day period. These countries include the United States, Canada, Australia, and many European countries. However, it's essential to check the latest visa requirements and exemptions based on your nationality.

- Schengen Area: The Czech Republic is a member of the Schengen Area. If you are required to obtain a visa, you will need to apply for a Schengen Visa, which allows travel within the entire Schengen Zone.
- Long-term Stays: If you plan to stay in the Czech Republic for more than 90 days or have a specific purpose such as work, study, or family reunification, you will need to apply for a long-term visa or residence permit before traveling to the country.
- Additional Documentation: When entering the Czech Republic, you may be asked to provide additional documents, such as proof of travel medical insurance, proof of

accommodation arrangements, proof of sufficient financial means to support yourself during your stay, and a return or onward ticket.

- COVID-19 Requirements: Due to the ongoing COVID-19 pandemic, additional entry requirements and restrictions may be in place. These may include providing proof of vaccination, negative COVID-19 test results, or undergoing quarantine upon arrival. It is crucial to check the latest travel advisories and requirements before your trip.

It's important to note that entry requirements can change, so it's advisable to consult the official website of the Czech embassy or consulate in your country or seek guidance from the nearest diplomatic mission to get the most up-to-date information regarding entry requirements.

Always ensure that you have the necessary documentation and meet the entry requirements before traveling to the Czech Republic to avoid any travel disruptions or issues at the border.

CHAPTER THREE: GETTING TO CZECH

Getting to the Czech Republic is relatively easy, thanks to its central location in Europe and well-connected transportation networks. Here are some recommended options for traveling to the Czech Republic:

By Air

The easiest and fastest way to reach the Czech Republic from international destinations is by air. The country has several international airports, with Václav Havel Airport Prague being the busiest and most well-connected. It serves as the main gateway for international travelers. Other airports, such as Brno-Turany Airport and Ostrava Leos Janacek Airport, also handle international flights, albeit on a smaller scale. Many major airlines operate regular flights to Prague from various cities around the world, making it convenient to reach the country.

By Train

Train travel to the Czech Republic is a popular option, especially if you're coming from neighboring European countries. Prague is well-connected to major European cities, and there are direct train services from Vienna, Berlin, Munich, and Warsaw, among others. Train travel offers a scenic and comfortable journey, allowing you to enjoy the picturesque landscapes along the way. The Czech Republic has an efficient and extensive rail network, making it easy to explore different regions of the country by train.

By Bus

Bus travel is another cost-effective option for reaching the Czech Republic, particularly for shorter distances or when traveling within Europe. Several bus companies operate international routes, connecting Prague and other major Czech cities to various European destinations. Bus travel can be a budget-friendly choice, and it provides flexibility in terms of routes and departure times.

By Car

If you prefer the freedom and flexibility of driving, reaching the Czech Republic by car is an option. The country has well-maintained road networks, and it is connected to neighboring countries through highways and border crossings. Driving to the Czech Republic allows you to explore the countryside and visit smaller towns and villages at your own pace. However, keep in mind that some cities, like Prague, have restricted driving zones, and parking can be challenging in popular tourist areas.

By Boat

Although the Czech Republic is landlocked, you can incorporate a river cruise into your travel plans. The Vltava River, which flows through Prague, is a popular route for river cruises that start or end in other European cities such as Budapest or Vienna. River cruises offer a unique perspective and allow you to enjoy the scenic beauty of the riverside landscapes.

When considering the best option to get to the Czech Republic, factors such as your location, budget, time available, and personal preferences will play a role. For international travelers, flying to Prague is often the most convenient and efficient choice. However, if you're already in Europe or prefer alternative modes of transportation, trains or buses can provide enjoyable and cost-effective travel experiences.

Whichever method you choose, arriving in the Czech Republic opens the door to a world of historical wonders, cultural treasures, and breathtaking landscapes that await your exploration.

CHAPTER FOUR: GETTING AROUND CZECH REPUBLIC

Transportation options

The Czech Republic offers a variety of transport options to help you navigate the country and explore its diverse regions. Here are the main transportation modes available:

Public Transportation:

Trains

Trains in the Czech Republic are a convenient and popular mode of transportation for both domestic and international travel. Here's everything you need to know about trains in the Czech Republic as a tourist:

Train Operators:

Czech Railways (České dráhy): The primary train operator in the Czech Republic, offering a comprehensive network of regional and long-distance trains.

RegioJet: A private train operator that offers both domestic and international connections, known for its modern fleet and amenities.

Train Types:

- InterCity (IC) and EuroCity (EC): These are higher-speed trains that connect major cities in the Czech Republic and beyond. They offer comfortable seating, onboard services, and often require seat reservations.
- Express (Ex): These are fast trains that connect major cities within the Czech Republic, offering a balance between speed and affordability.
- Regional (Os, Sp, R): Regional trains serve shorter distances, connecting smaller towns and villages within a specific region. These trains are slower but offer a more extensive network and flexibility.

Train Tickets and Prices:

Train tickets can be purchased at train stations, online, or at ticket machines. Online booking platforms like Czech Railways' eShop or RegioJet's website allow you to purchase tickets in advance.

Ticket prices vary depending on the distance, train type, and class. Generally, regional trains are more affordable compared to IC or EC trains. Prices for shorter trips can range from around 50 CZK ($2) to 200 CZK ($9), while longer trips can cost between 200 CZK ($9) and 800 CZK ($36) or more.

Discounts are available for seniors, students, and children, so be sure to check if you qualify for any reduced fares.

Train Stations:

Major train stations in the Czech Republic include Prague Main Station (Praha Hlavní nádraží), Brno Main Station (Brno hlavní nádraží), Ostrava Main Station (Ostrava hlavní nádraží), and Plzeň Main Station (Plzeň hlavní nádraží). These stations offer various facilities such as ticket counters, information desks, luggage storage, and dining options.

Working Hours:

Train services in the Czech Republic generally operate from early morning until midnight. However, specific schedules may vary depending on the route and train type.

Major train stations are typically open throughout the day, providing access to ticket counters, waiting areas, and facilities. Smaller stations may have more limited operating hours.

Seat Reservations:

Seat reservations are required for some InterCity (IC) and EuroCity (EC) trains. It is advisable to make reservations, especially during peak travel periods or if you prefer a specific seat.

Reservations can be made at train stations or online, and there is usually a small fee for reserving a seat.

Additional Tips:

Arrive at the train station at least 15 minutes before the departure time to allow for ticket purchase and boarding.

Validate your ticket using the yellow ticket validation machines before boarding regional trains.

Keep your ticket with you throughout the journey, as ticket inspections are common.

It's worth noting that train travel in the Czech Republic offers scenic views of the countryside and comfortable journeys. Whether you're traveling between major cities, exploring smaller towns, or venturing into neighboring countries, the train system provides a reliable and efficient way to get around and enjoy the beauty of the Czech Republic.

Buses

Buses are a popular and convenient mode of transportation in the Czech Republic, offering extensive domestic and international connections. Here's everything you need to know about buses in the Czech Republic as a tourist:

Bus Operators:

- FlixBus: A major bus company operating both domestic and international routes with a large network of destinations.
- RegioJet: A private bus operator offering domestic and international connections, known for its modern fleet and comfortable amenities.
- Student Agency: Another popular bus operator providing domestic and international services.

Bus Types:

- Intercity Buses: These buses connect major cities and towns within the Czech Republic, as well as neighboring countries. They offer comfortable seating and onboard amenities such as Wi-Fi and power outlets.

- Regional Buses: Regional buses serve shorter distances, connecting smaller towns and villages within specific regions. They are more frequent but may have fewer amenities compared to intercity buses.

Bus Tickets and Prices:

Bus tickets can be purchased online through the respective bus company's website, mobile apps, or at designated ticket counters at bus stations.

Prices vary depending on the distance and the operator. Generally, prices for shorter trips within the Czech Republic range from around 50 CZK ($2) to 300 CZK ($14). Longer trips to neighboring countries or farther destinations can cost between 300 CZK ($14) and 800 CZK ($36) or more.

Discounts for seniors, students, and children may be available, so it's worth checking if you qualify for reduced fares.

Bus Stations:

Major cities have central bus stations, such as Prague Florenc, Brno Zvonařka, and Ostrava Central Bus Station. These stations provide facilities like ticket counters, waiting areas, restrooms, and sometimes shops or cafés.

Smaller towns may have smaller bus stations or stops, which can vary in terms of available amenities.

Working Hours:

Bus services operate throughout the day, with varying frequencies depending on the route and time of day.

Major bus stations are usually open during regular business hours, while smaller stations may have more limited operating hours.

Additional Tips:

Arrive at the bus station a few minutes before the departure time to allow for ticket purchase and boarding.

Some buses may require a printed ticket, so it's advisable to check the requirements during the booking process.

Keep your ticket with you throughout the journey, as ticket inspections may occur.

Buses offer flexibility, affordable fares, and a wide network of destinations, making them a popular choice for travel within the Czech Republic and neighboring countries. Whether you're exploring the bustling streets of Prague or venturing into the scenic countryside, buses provide a reliable and comfortable way to get around and discover the beauty of the Czech Republic.

Trams and Metro

Trams and metro systems in the Czech Republic provide efficient and convenient transportation options, especially within major cities. Here's everything you need to know about trams and metro in the Czech Republic:

Trams:

Tram Networks: Major cities like Prague, Brno, Ostrava, and Pilsen have well-developed tram networks that cover extensive areas within the city.

Tickets: Tram tickets can be purchased at ticket vending machines located at tram stops or at selected kiosks. Some cities also offer options for mobile ticketing through smartphone apps.

Ticket Validation: Before boarding the tram, make sure to validate your ticket using the yellow ticket validation machines located inside the tram or at tram stops.

Operating Hours: Trams usually operate from early morning until midnight, although specific schedules may vary depending on the city and tram line. Some cities may have night trams that operate during late hours or offer limited service.

Metro:

- Metro Systems: Prague, the capital city of the Czech Republic, has a well-developed metro system consisting of three lines: Line A (Green), Line B (Yellow), and Line C (Red). The metro is the fastest and most convenient way to travel within Prague.
- Tickets: Metro tickets can be purchased at ticket vending machines located at metro stations or at selected kiosks. It's important to validate your ticket before entering the metro platform using the yellow ticket validation machines.
- Operating Hours: Prague Metro operates from early morning until midnight, with trains running at regular intervals. During weekends and holidays, the metro operates at slightly reduced frequencies.

Tickets and Fares:

- Ticket Types: Trams and metro generally have common ticket systems within each city. Single ride tickets, timed tickets (valid for a specific duration), or day passes are usually available.
- Fare Zones: In some cities, the fare system is divided into zones, and the ticket price may depend on the number of zones traveled. Make sure to purchase the appropriate ticket based on your intended journey.
- Fare Validation: It's important to carry a validated ticket throughout your journey, as ticket inspections are conducted randomly, and penalties can be issued for traveling without a valid ticket.

Additional Tips:

Tram and metro maps are readily available at tram stops, metro stations, or online. They provide an overview of the network, lines, and stations to help you plan your journey.

Be mindful of pickpocketing, especially in crowded trams and metro trains. Keep an eye on your possessions and make sure they're safe.

Trams and metro systems are well-integrated with other forms of public transportation, allowing you to transfer between trams, metro, and buses using the same ticket.

Using trams and metro in the Czech Republic offers a convenient and efficient way to explore cities and reach popular attractions. Whether you're wandering through the historic streets of Prague or navigating the vibrant neighborhoods of Brno, trams and metro systems provide reliable and hassle-free transportation options for both residents and tourists alike.

Taxis are a convenient mode of transportation in the Czech Republic, offering flexibility and door-to-door service. Here's everything you need to know about taking taxis in the Czech Republic as a tourist:

Taxi Availability:

Taxis can be found in cities, towns, and popular tourist areas. Look for taxi stands (identified by the "Taxi" sign) or hail a taxi on the street. Taxis can also be booked through ride-hailing apps like Uber or Bolt, which operate in some Czech cities.

Licensed Taxis:

It is advisable to use licensed taxis to ensure a safe and reliable service. Look for taxis with official markings, such as a taxi sign on the roof, a company logo, or a license number on the vehicle.

Pricing and Payment:

Taxis in the Czech Republic usually operate on a metered system. The cost is determined by the distance traveled and the amount of time spent in the cab.

Make sure the meter is running from the start of the journey. If the taxi doesn't have a meter, agree on the fare in advance.

Additional charges may apply for luggage, traveling during late hours, or using taxis at the airport.

Taxis accept cash, and some may also accept credit/debit cards. It's advisable to carry some cash for payment, especially for shorter rides.

Taxi Apps:

Ride-hailing apps like Uber and Bolt operate in certain Czech cities, providing an alternative to traditional taxis. These apps allow you to book and pay for rides conveniently using your smartphone.

Additional Tips:

It's helpful to have the name and address of your destination written down or saved on your phone in case of language barriers.

Always ensure that the driver resets the meter before the start of the journey.

If you have any concerns about the fare or the service, ask for a receipt (potvrzení) that includes the taxi company's name and contact information.

Keep an eye on your belongings during the taxi ride to prevent theft or loss.

Using taxis in the Czech Republic offers convenience and accessibility, especially when traveling with heavy luggage or navigating unfamiliar areas. While most taxi drivers provide a reliable and honest service, it's always a good idea to exercise caution and choose licensed taxis to ensure a safe and fair experience.

Rental Cars

Renting a car in the Czech Republic can be a great option for exploring the country at your own pace and accessing more remote areas. Here's everything you need to know about renting a car in the Czech Republic as a tourist:

Rental Car Companies:

Major international car rental companies like Hertz, Avis, Europcar, and Budget operate in the Czech Republic. They have rental offices at major airports, train stations, and in city centers.

Local car rental companies also offer services, providing additional options for rental vehicles.

Requirements:

- Age: The minimum age requirement for renting a car in the Czech Republic is typically 21 years, although some companies may require renters to be 25 or older. Young drivers could be subject to extra charges or limitations.

- Driver's License: You must have a valid driver's license from your home country or an International Driving Permit (IDP) if your license is not in English or another widely recognized language.
- Insurance: Rental cars usually come with basic insurance coverage. It's advisable to consider additional insurance options, such as collision damage waiver (CDW) or theft protection, to minimize your liability in case of accidents or theft.

Booking and Rental Process:

- Booking: It's recommended to book your rental car in advance, especially during peak travel seasons, to ensure availability and secure better rates.
- Rental Agreement: When picking up the rental car, you'll be required to sign a rental agreement, which outlines the terms and conditions of the rental, including fuel policy, mileage limits, and any additional fees.

- Inspection: Conduct a thorough inspection of the car before accepting it, noting any existing damages or issues on the rental agreement. Taking photos or videos can serve as evidence if needed.

Road Rules and Driving in the Czech Republic:

- Driving Side: Drive on the right side of the road in the Czech Republic.
- Speed Limits: Speed limits are typically 50 km/h (31 mph) in residential areas, 90 km/h (56 mph) on regular roads, and 130 km/h (80 mph) on highways.
- Seat Belts: Seat belts are mandatory for both the driver and all passengers.
- Alcohol Limit: The legal blood alcohol concentration limit is 0.0%, meaning no alcohol is allowed while driving.
- Toll Roads: Some highways in the Czech Republic require payment of tolls. Make sure to familiarize yourself with the toll system and have appropriate payment methods.

Parking:

Parking in the Czech Republic is regulated in most cities. Look for designated parking areas, parking garages, or pay-and-display parking zones. There can be time limitations or parking permits needed in certain regions.

Fuel:

Gasoline (benzín) and diesel (nafta) are the most common types of fuel available at gas stations. Unleaded petrol (95 or 98 octane) is widely available.

Renting a car in the Czech Republic allows you to explore the country's charming towns, picturesque landscapes, and off-the-beaten-path destinations. Ensure you have a valid driver's license, understand the local road rules, and choose a rental company that meets your needs to make the most of your driving experience in the Czech Republic.

Cycling

Cycling is a popular and enjoyable way to explore the Czech Republic, offering the opportunity to discover the country's beautiful landscapes, charming towns, and cultural sites. Here's everything you need to know about cycling in the Czech Republic as a tourist:

Cycling Infrastructure:

Cycle Paths and Routes: The Czech Republic has a well-developed cycling infrastructure, with a network of cycle paths and routes that cover both urban areas and rural regions. Many cities, including Prague, Brno, and Ostrava, have designated cycling lanes within city limits.

Czech Greenways: The Czech Greenways are a series of scenic cycling routes that connect various regions of the country. They offer a combination of well-marked paths, quiet roads, and off-road sections, allowing cyclists to explore the Czech Republic's countryside and cultural heritage.

Bike Rental:

Bike Rental Shops: Many cities and tourist destinations in the Czech Republic have bike rental shops where you can rent bicycles for a few hours or even several days. Depending on the model of bike and the length of the rental, different prices apply.

Bike-Sharing: Some cities, such as Prague, offer bike-sharing programs where you can rent bikes for short periods. These bikes can be picked up and dropped off at designated stations throughout the city.

Cycling Routes and Trails:

Czech Republic Cycle Trails: The Czech Republic boasts numerous cycling routes and trails suitable for different levels of cycling proficiency. These routes often pass through scenic countryside, forests, and cultural landmarks.

EuroVelo Routes: The Czech Republic is part of the EuroVelo network, which consists of long-distance cycling routes connecting various European countries. EuroVelo Route 7 (Sun Route) and EuroVelo Route 13 (Iron Curtain Trail) pass through the Czech Republic, offering diverse cycling experiences.

Safety and Regulations:

Safety Gear: It is recommended to wear a helmet while cycling, although it is not mandatory for adults in the Czech Republic.

Road Rules: Cyclists must follow the same traffic rules as motorists, including observing traffic lights and signs.

Bike Security: Ensure your bicycle is securely locked when not in use, especially in crowded areas or overnight.

Cycling Etiquette:

Be considerate of pedestrians and other cyclists, especially in shared spaces.

Use hand signals to indicate your intentions, such as turning or stopping.

Stay on designated cycling paths or use the right-hand side of the road when cycling on the road.

Bike-Friendly Facilities:

Bike-Friendly Accommodation: Many accommodations, particularly in tourist areas, offer facilities for storing bicycles securely.

Repair Shops: In case of any mechanical issues, there are bike repair shops available in cities and towns where you can get assistance and repair services.

Exploring the Czech Republic by bike allows you to connect with nature, immerse yourself in the local culture, and enjoy the country's scenic beauty at a leisurely pace. Whether you're pedaling through historical towns, following cycling routes through picturesque countryside, or cycling along riverbanks

Domestic Flight

Domestic flights in the Czech Republic offer a convenient and time-saving option for traveling longer distances within the country. Here's everything you need to know about domestic flights as a tourist:

Domestic Airports:

Václav Havel Airport Prague (PRG): Prague's international airport also serves as the main hub for domestic flights. Several domestic airlines operate from this airport, providing connections to other cities within the Czech Republic.

Brno-Turany Airport (BRQ): Located in Brno, this airport offers domestic flights to and from Prague and other destinations.

Ostrava Leos Janacek Airport (OSR): Situated in Ostrava, this airport provides domestic flights primarily to and from Prague.

Airlines:

Czech Airlines (České aerolinie): The national carrier of the Czech Republic, Czech Airlines offers domestic flights connecting Prague with Brno and Ostrava.

Smartwings: Smartwings is a Czech low-cost airline that operates domestic flights between Prague and several other cities within the country.

Booking Flights:

Flight Tickets: Domestic flight tickets can be booked online through airline websites or through travel agencies. It's advisable to book in advance, especially during peak travel seasons, to secure better fares and ensure availability.

Check-In: Domestic flights generally require passengers to check in at the airport before departure. Check the specific requirements and recommended check-in times provided by the airline.

Flight Duration and Routes:

Domestic flights within the Czech Republic are relatively short, with flight durations typically ranging from 30 minutes to 1 hour.

The most common route is between Prague and other major cities like Brno and Ostrava. Flights between Prague and regional airports offer quick access to different parts of the country.

Airport Facilities:

Domestic airports in the Czech Republic offer standard facilities, including check-in counters, baggage handling services, boarding gates, and car rental services.

 Arrive at the airport long before your flight's departure time to allow for check-in, security procedures, and any unexpected delays.

Additional Tips:

Baggage Allowance: Check the baggage allowance provided by the airline as it may vary depending on the ticket type or fare class.

Flight Delays or Cancellations: Like any other flight, domestic flights may experience delays or cancellations due to weather conditions or other unforeseen circumstances. Stay informed through airline announcements or notifications and make necessary adjustments to your travel plans if needed.

Domestic flights in the Czech Republic offer a convenient option for reaching different parts of the country quickly. They are particularly beneficial when time is limited or when you need to cover longer distances. By taking advantage of domestic flights, you can maximize your time and explore the various regions of the Czech Republic efficiently.

Ferries

Ferries may not be the most common mode of transportation in the Czech Republic since the country is landlocked. However, there are a few opportunities for ferry travel on certain rivers and lakes. Here's what you need to know about ferries in the Czech Republic:

Vltava River Ferries:

Prague: In Prague, the Vltava River offers ferry services that provide a scenic way to travel and explore different parts of the city. These ferry services operate within Prague and can take you to popular destinations such as Prague Castle, Charles Bridge, and the Prague Zoo.

Melnik: Located about 30 kilometers north of Prague, the town of Melnik is situated at the confluence of the Vltava and Elbe rivers. From Melnik, you can take a river ferry that connects to the nearby town of Litomerice, providing a picturesque journey along the rivers.

Lipno Lake Ferries:

Lipno Lake: Located in South Bohemia, Lipno Lake is the largest lake in the Czech Republic. Ferry services operate on the lake, connecting various points and providing a pleasant way to enjoy the surrounding natural beauty. The ferries offer transportation for both passengers and bicycles.

Sailing Trips:

Some travel companies or private operators may offer sailing trips or cruises on rivers or lakes in the Czech Republic. These trips can provide a unique way to explore the country's waterways and enjoy the scenic landscapes.

It's important to note that the availability and schedules of ferry services may vary depending on the season and weather conditions. It's advisable to check the operating hours, routes, and any specific requirements or restrictions related to the ferry services before planning your journey.

While ferry travel may not be as extensive in the Czech Republic as in coastal regions, the opportunities to experience scenic boat trips on rivers and lakes can provide a refreshing perspective and add an extra dimension to your exploration of the country's waterways.

CHAPTER FIVE: ACCOMMODATIONS OPTIONS

Top five hotels

Here are five top hotels in the Czech Republic, each with their amenity properties, room features, room types, and approximate price ranges. Please note that prices can vary depending on the season and availability.

1. **Augustine, a Luxury Collection Hotel, Prague - Prague**

Amenities: Spa and wellness center, fitness center, restaurant, bar, terrace, garden, concierge service.

Room Features: Air conditioning, flat-screen TV, minibar, safe, complimentary Wi-Fi, luxurious bedding, en-suite bathroom with bathrobes and slippers.

Room Types: Deluxe Room, Junior Suite, Signature Suite, Executive Suite, Royal Suite.

Price Range: Starting from approximately 3000 CZK ($133) per night.

2. The Emblem Hotel - Prague

Amenities: Rooftop terrace with a Jacuzzi, fitness center, spa and wellness facilities, restaurant, bar, library, 24-hour front desk.

Room Features: Air conditioning, flat-screen TV, minibar, coffee machine, safe, complimentary Wi-Fi, luxurious bedding, marble bathroom with bathrobes and slippers.

Room Types: Deluxe Room, Grand Deluxe Room, Junior Suite, Emblem Suite, Penthouse Suite.

Price Range: Starting from approximately 4000 CZK ($178) per night.

3. Hotel Imperial - Karlovy Vary

Amenities: Spa and wellness center, indoor swimming pool, fitness center, restaurant, bar, terrace, garden, concierge service.

Room Features: Air conditioning, flat-screen TV, minibar, safe, complimentary Wi-Fi, seating area, en-suite bathroom with bathrobes and slippers.

Room Types: Superior Room, Deluxe Room, Executive Room, Suite.

Price Range: Starting from approximately 2500 CZK ($111) per night.

4. Alchymist Grand Hotel and Spa - Prague

Amenities: Spa and wellness center, indoor pool, fitness center, restaurant, bar, terrace, garden, concierge service.

Room Features: Air conditioning, flat-screen TV, minibar, safe, complimentary Wi-Fi, luxurious bedding, seating area, en-suite marble bathroom with bathrobes and slippers.

Room Types: Superior Room, Deluxe Room, Junior Suite, One-Bedroom Suite, Presidential Suite.

Price Range: Starting from approximately 5000 CZK ($222) per night.

5. Mariánské Lázn's Esplanade Spa and Golf Resort

Amenities: Spa and wellness center, outdoor and indoor pools, golf course, tennis court, fitness center, restaurant, bar, terrace, garden, concierge service.

Room Features: Air conditioning, flat-screen TV, minibar, safe, complimentary Wi-Fi, seating area, en-suite bathroom with bathrobes and slippers.

Room Types: Superior Room, Deluxe Room, Junior Suite, Executive Suite.

Price Range: Starting from approximately 3500 CZK ($155) per night.

These hotels offer a range of amenities, luxurious room features, and different price points to cater to various preferences and budgets. When making a reservation, be sure to check the specific room availability, rates, and any special offers or packages provided by the hotel.

Top Five Hostels

Here are five hostels in the Czech Republic, each with their amenities, room types, and approximate price ranges. Hostels are a more budget-friendly accommodation option that often provide shared dormitory-style rooms and communal spaces for travelers.

1. **Hostel One Prague - Prague**

Amenities: Common lounge area, fully equipped kitchen, free breakfast, organized social activities, 24-hour reception, free Wi-Fi, laundry facilities.

Room Types: Mixed or female-only dormitory rooms with bunk beds.

Price Range: Starting from approximately 300 CZK ($13) per person per night.

2. **Mosaic House - Prague**

Amenities: Bar and lounge, café, restaurant, terrace, fully equipped kitchen, free breakfast, organized events, 24-hour reception, free Wi-Fi, laundry facilities.

Room Types: Mixed or female-only dormitory rooms with bunk beds, private rooms with shared or en-suite bathrooms.

Price Range: Starting from approximately 400 CZK ($18) per person per night.

3. Sir Toby's Hostel - Prague

Amenities: Bar and common room, fully equipped kitchen, free breakfast, garden, terrace, organized events, 24-hour reception, free Wi-Fi, laundry facilities.

Room Types: Mixed or female-only dormitory rooms with bunk beds, private rooms with shared or en-suite bathrooms.

Price Range: Starting from approximately 250 CZK ($11) per person per night.

4. Hostel Santini Prague - Prague

Amenities: Lounge area, fully equipped kitchen, free breakfast, rooftop terrace, 24-hour reception, free Wi-Fi, laundry facilities.

Room Types: Mixed or female-only dormitory rooms with bunk beds, private rooms with shared or en-suite bathrooms.

Price Range: Starting from approximately 350 CZK ($16) per person per night.

5. Hostel 99 - Český Krumlov

Amenities: Common lounge area, fully equipped kitchen, terrace, free Wi-Fi, 24-hour reception, luggage storage.

Room Types: Mixed or female-only dormitory rooms with bunk beds, private rooms with shared or en-suite bathrooms.

Price Range: Starting from approximately 250 CZK ($11) per person per night.

These hostels offer affordable accommodation options for travelers and provide essential amenities to ensure a comfortable stay. Prices can vary depending on the season and availability.

Top Five Vacation Rentals

Here are five top vacation rentals in the Czech Republic, each with their amenity properties, room features, room types, and approximate price ranges. Vacation rentals offer a more independent and private accommodation option for travelers.

1. **Prague Old Town Boutique Apartments - Prague**

Amenities: Fully equipped kitchen, living area, free Wi-Fi, air conditioning, laundry facilities, 24-hour check-in.

Room Features: One or two bedrooms, private bathroom, spacious living and dining area.

Price Range: Starting from approximately 1500 CZK ($67) per night.

2. **Karlovy Vary Apartment - Karlovy Vary**

Amenities: Fully equipped kitchen, living area, free Wi-Fi, balcony or terrace, laundry facilities.

Room Features: One or two bedrooms, private bathroom, separate living and dining area.

Price Range: Starting from approximately 2000 CZK ($89) per night.

3. Esk Krumlov Luxury Apartment - Esk Krumlov

Amenities: Fully equipped kitchen, living area, free Wi-Fi, balcony or terrace, laundry facilities.

Room Features: One or two bedrooms, private bathroom, spacious living and dining area.

Price Range: Starting from approximately 2500 CZK ($111) per night.

4. Charming Villa in the Bohemian Countryside - Rural location

Amenities: Fully equipped kitchen, living area, free Wi-Fi, garden or outdoor space, barbecue facilities.

Room Features: Multiple bedrooms, private bathrooms, cozy living and dining area.

Price Range: Starting from approximately 3000 CZK ($133) per night.

5. Luxury Lakefront Cabin in Lipno - Lipno nad Vltavou

Amenities: Fully equipped kitchen, living area, free Wi-Fi, terrace or balcony, lake access, sauna or hot tub.

Room Features: Multiple bedrooms, private bathrooms, spacious living and dining area.

Price Range: Starting from approximately 4000 CZK ($178) per night.

These vacation rentals offer comfortable and private spaces for travelers, allowing them to enjoy their stay with added convenience and flexibility. Prices can vary depending on the season, location, and availability, so it's advisable to check the property's official website or booking platforms for the most up-to-date rates and availability.

Here are five top Bed and Breakfast (B&B) establishments in the Czech Republic, each with their amenity properties, room features, room types, and approximate price ranges. B&Bs offer a cozy and personalized accommodation experience with a hearty breakfast included.

1. Golden Key - Prague

Amenities: Breakfast included, free Wi-Fi, concierge service, garden or terrace, 24-hour front desk.

Room Features: En-suite bathroom, TV, safe, minibar, tea/coffee making facilities.

Room Types: Single Room, Double Room, Triple Room, Family Room.

Price Range: Starting from approximately 1500 CZK ($67) per night.

2. Pension U Lilie - Český Krumlov

Amenities: Breakfast included, free Wi-Fi, garden, terrace, 24-hour front desk.

Room Features: En-suite bathroom, TV, seating area, tea/coffee making facilities.

Room Types: Double Room, Triple Room, Quadruple Room.

Price Range: Starting from approximately 1800 CZK ($80) per night.

3. Pension Atelier 12 - Karlovy Vary

Amenities: Breakfast included, free Wi-Fi, garden, terrace, shared lounge, 24-hour front desk.

Room Features: En-suite bathroom, TV, seating area, tea/coffee making facilities.

Room Types: Double Room, Triple Room.

Price Range: Starting from approximately 2000 CZK ($89) per night.

4. Pension U Zámku - České Budějovice

Amenities: Breakfast included, free Wi-Fi, garden, terrace, shared lounge, 24-hour front desk.

Room Features: En-suite bathroom, TV, seating area, tea/coffee making facilities.

Room Types: Double Room, Triple Room.

Price Range: Starting from approximately 1700 CZK ($76) per night.

5. Villa Basileia - Brno

Amenities: Breakfast included, free Wi-Fi, garden, terrace, shared lounge, 24-hour front desk.

Room Features: En-suite bathroom, TV, seating area, tea/coffee making facilities.

Room Types: Double Room, Twin Room, Triple Room.

Price Range: Starting from approximately 2000 CZK ($89) per night.

These B&Bs offer a warm and welcoming atmosphere, along with comfortable rooms and a delicious breakfast to start your day. Prices can vary depending on the season, location, and availability

CHAPTER SIX: TOP ATTRACTIONS

Kutná Hora

This UNESCO World Heritage site is known for its remarkable architectural landmarks. The most famous is the Sedlec Ossuary, also known as the Bone Church, which features a unique interior adorned with human bones. The stunning St. Barbara's Church and the Italian Court are other must-visit attractions in Kutná Hora.

Český Krumlov

Located in southern Bohemia, Český Krumlov is a beautifully preserved medieval town with a picturesque castle complex. Wander through its narrow cobblestone streets, visit the stunning Český Krumlov Castle, and take a scenic boat ride along the Vltava River that surrounds the town.

Telč

Telč is a small town renowned for its well-preserved Renaissance architecture. The main attraction is the Telč Castle, featuring beautiful facades and a picturesque pond. The town's historic center, lined with colorful Renaissance and Gothic houses, is a UNESCO World Heritage site.

Karlovy Vary

This renowned spa town is famous for its hot springs and elegant architecture. Relax in the healing mineral waters, stroll along the colonnades, and indulge in spa treatments. Don't miss the iconic Grandhotel Pupp, known for its appearances in movies like James Bond's "Casino Royale."

Olomouc

Olomouc is a historic city in Moravia, known for its charming squares, stunning architecture, and vibrant student atmosphere. Visit the UNESCO-listed Holy Trinity Column, explore the beautiful Archbishop's Palace, and wander through the main square with its astronomical clock and fountains.

Pilsen

Beer enthusiasts should not miss a visit to Pilsen, the birthplace of the famous Pilsner beer. Take a tour of the Pilsner Urquell Brewery, learn about the beer-making process, and sample the renowned Czech lagers. The city also boasts a charming historic center and the impressive St. Bartholomew's Cathedral.

Třebíč

Třebíč is known for its Jewish Quarter, a UNESCO World Heritage site. Explore the Jewish Quarter with its synagogue, Jewish cemetery, and well-preserved houses. The Basilica of St. Procopius, a Romanesque-Gothic masterpiece, is another highlight of the city.

Bohemian Switzerland National Park

Located in the north of the country, this national park is a paradise for nature lovers. Admire the breathtaking sandstone formations, hike through picturesque gorges, and visit the iconic Pravčická Gate, the largest natural sandstone arch in Europe.

These attractions offer a glimpse into the rich history, cultural heritage, and natural beauty of the Czech Republic. From architectural marvels to natural wonders, each destination has its own unique charm, inviting you to delve deeper into the country's diverse and captivating offerings.

CHAPTER SEVEN: DINNING AND NIGHT LIFE

Local Cuisines

Czech cuisine is known for its hearty and flavorful dishes that reflect the country's rich culinary heritage. Influenced by both Central European and Slavic traditions, Czech cuisine offers a range of delicious and satisfying options. Here are some popular local Czech dishes to try:

Svíčková na Smetaně: This classic Czech dish consists of marinated beef sirloin, slow-cooked in a creamy vegetable sauce, and served with bread dumplings (knedlíky) and a dollop of sour cream. The sauce is made with root vegetables, spices, and often includes a hint of lemon zest for added flavor.

Vepřo-knedlo-zelo: A beloved Czech dish, it features roasted pork (vepřová pečeně) served with bread dumplings (knedlíky) and braised cabbage (zelí). The pork is typically marinated and slow-cooked to tender perfection, while the dumplings and cabbage add texture and flavor to the dish.

Guláš: Czech-style goulash is a hearty meat stew, typically made with tender beef, onions, paprika, and other spices. It is slow-cooked until the meat is tender and the flavors are well-infused. It is often served with bread or bread dumplings.

Trdelník: A popular Czech sweet treat, trdelník is a cylindrical pastry made from rolled dough that is wrapped around a wooden dowel, grilled, and coated with sugar and sometimes cinnamon. It is commonly enjoyed as a warm, crispy, and indulgent street food dessert.

Smažený Sýr: Known as fried cheese, this dish features a slice of cheese, usually Edam or Hermelín, coated in breadcrumbs and deep-fried until golden and crispy. It is typically served with tartar sauce and a side of fries or salad.

Bramboráky: These potato pancakes are a Czech specialty made from grated potatoes, flour, eggs, and seasonings. They are pan-fried until golden and served with sour cream or applesauce. Bramboráky are often enjoyed as a delicious snack or a side dish.

Utopenci: Utopenci, meaning "drowned men," are pickled sausages typically served as a popular pub snack in the Czech Republic. The sausages are marinated in a mixture of vinegar, onions, garlic, spices, and sometimes chili peppers, resulting in a tangy and flavorful bite.

Koláče: These Czech pastries come in various shapes and flavors, typically with a sweet yeast dough base filled with fruit preserves, poppy seeds, or a sweet cheese filling. Koláče are a popular choice for breakfast or as a sweet treat with coffee.

When visiting the Czech Republic, exploring the local cuisine is an essential part of experiencing the country's culture. Whether you're savoring hearty meat dishes, indulging in sweet pastries, or enjoying traditional street food, Czech cuisine offers a range of flavors and textures that will delight your taste buds. Don't forget to pair your meal with a glass of excellent Czech beer, as the country is renowned for its brewing tradition.

Top Five Restaurants

1. Lokál: Lokál is a popular chain of Czech restaurants with several branches in Prague and one in Pilsen. The lively and bustling atmosphere resembles a traditional pub, with long wooden tables and a convivial ambiance. Lokál is known for serving authentic Czech dishes made from locally sourced ingredients. Their menu features classics such as svíčková (marinated beef sirloin), goulash, and crispy pork knuckle. Prices at Lokál are affordable, with main courses ranging from 100 CZK ($4.50) to 250 CZK ($11). It's advisable to arrive early or make a reservation, as Lokál can get quite busy during peak hours.

2. U Kroka: Located in Prague's Nusle district, U Kroka is a charming Czech restaurant with a cozy and welcoming atmosphere. The interior showcases rustic decor, including wooden beams and traditional furnishings. U Kroka

specializes in serving hearty Czech cuisine, offering a wide selection of dishes such as roasted meats, schnitzels, and traditional soups like kulajda (a creamy potato and mushroom soup). The prices at U Kroka are budget-friendly, with main courses typically ranging from 150 CZK ($7) to 250 CZK ($11). The restaurant is popular among locals and visitors alike, so it's recommended to make a reservation, especially during peak dining hours.

3. Krčma: Situated in the picturesque town of Český Krumlov, Krčma is a traditional Czech restaurant that captures the essence of South Bohemian cuisine. The restaurant's cozy interior features wooden beams, rustic furnishings, and a warm atmosphere. Krčma specializes in local delicacies such as roasted duck, pork knuckle, and traditional dumplings served with various sauces. The menu also includes vegetarian options. Prices for main courses at Krčma typically range from 150 CZK

($7) to 300 CZK ($14), making it an affordable choice for enjoying authentic Czech cuisine in a charming setting.

4. **Hospůdka u Kmotra**: Located in Prague's Vinohrady district, Hospůdka u Kmotra is a friendly and laid-back pub-style restaurant that offers a taste of Czech comfort food. The interior exudes a casual and welcoming vibe with wooden tables, vintage beer signs, and a lively atmosphere. The menu features a range of Czech dishes, including goulash, schnitzels, grilled meats, and traditional side dishes like potato salad or sauerkraut. The prices for main courses at Hospůdka u Kmotra typically range from 150 CZK ($7) to 250 CZK ($11). It's advisable to arrive early or make a reservation, especially during peak dining hours.

5. **Restaurace Mlejnice**: With branches in Prague's Old Town and Lesser Town, Restaurace Mlejnice is a popular restaurant that offers a casual and relaxed atmosphere.

The interior showcases rustic elements, including stone walls and wooden beams. Restaurace Mlejnice is known for its grilled meat dishes, including skewers, mixed grills, and a variety of sauces and sides. The menu also features other Czech specialties like goulash and fried cheese. The prices for main courses at Restaurace Mlejnice typically range from 150 CZK ($7) to 250 CZK ($11). It's recommended to arrive early or make a reservation, especially during busy times.

When visiting these budget-friendly restaurants in the Czech Republic, keep in mind:

Czech restaurants often operate on a self-service basis. You may need to order and pay at the counter or directly from the staff. Some places may give you a receipt, which you take to the counter to settle the bill.

Cash is widely accepted, although some restaurants may also accept credit or debit cards. It's always a good idea to have some cash on hand.

Tipping is customary in Czech restaurants. A tip of around 10% of the total bill is appreciated for good service. You can leave the tip in cash on the table or inform the staff of the amount you wish to add to the payment.

These affordable restaurants provide an excellent opportunity to savor traditional Czech cuisine without straining your budget. Enjoy the cozy atmospheres, sample delicious dishes, and immerse yourself in the local dining culture during your visit to the Czech Republic.

Top Five Bars Stations

Here are five affordable bars in the Czech Republic where tourists can enjoy a drink without breaking the bank. Please note that prices are approximate and may vary.

U Sudu - Prague: U Sudu is a unique and quirky underground bar located in Prague's Old Town. The bar is spread across multiple interconnected cellars, each with its own atmosphere. It offers a wide selection of Czech beers on tap and a variety of other drinks. Prices for beer range from 35 CZK ($1.50) to 60 CZK ($2.50), depending on the brand and size of the beer. The bar often gets crowded, especially in the evenings, so arriving early is recommended to secure a spot.

Vinárna U Křížů - Brno: Vinárna U Křížů is a cozy wine bar located in the city of Brno. It offers an extensive selection of Czech wines, along with a few international options. The bar has a relaxed and welcoming atmosphere, making it an ideal spot to unwind. Prices for a glass of wine range from 40

CZK ($1.75) to 90 CZK ($4), depending on the wine selection. The bar also serves light snacks to complement the wines.

Pivovar U Tří Růží - Prague: Pivovar U Tří Růží is a small brewery and pub located in Prague's New Town. It specializes in crafting their own traditional Czech beers on-site. Visitors can enjoy a pint of freshly brewed beer for approximately 40 CZK ($1.75) to 50 CZK ($2.25). The pub has a cozy interior with a friendly atmosphere, offering a taste of Czech beer culture.

Lokál - Prague: Lokál, mentioned earlier as a restaurant, also features a lively bar atmosphere. The pub serves a variety of Czech beers, both on tap and in bottles, offering a great opportunity to try different local brews. Prices for beer range from 35 CZK ($1.50) to 70 CZK ($3), depending on the type and size of the beer. The bustling pub atmosphere makes it a popular spot among locals and tourists alike.

U Fleků - Prague: U Fleků is a historic brewery and beer hall located in Prague's New Town. It has been brewing beer for over 500 years and is a beloved institution in the city. U Fleků serves its renowned dark lager, which is a must-try for beer enthusiasts. Prices for beer start at around 70 CZK ($3) for a half-liter. The beer hall also features live music and traditional Czech cuisine.

When visiting these bars in the Czech Republic, keep the following tips in mind:

Czech pubs often accept cash only, so it's advisable to have some cash on hand.

Tipping is customary in bars. It's typical to round up the bill or leave a small tip of around 10% of the total amount.

Smoking is prohibited in indoor public places, including bars and restaurants, with designated smoking areas available outside.

These affordable bars provide an opportunity to experience Czech beer culture and enjoy a drink in a lively and relaxed atmosphere. Immerse yourself in the local pub scene, try different beers, and mingle with locals and fellow travelers during your visit to the Czech Republic.

Top five nightlife places

Here are five vibrant nightlife spots in the Czech Republic where tourists can enjoy a lively evening. Please note that prices can vary, and it's always a good idea to check current rates and opening hours before visiting.

Roxy - Prague: Roxy is a renowned nightclub located in the heart of Prague's Old Town. It features multiple floors with different music genres, including electronic, indie, and alternative. The club hosts regular DJ events and live music performances, attracting a diverse crowd. Entrance fees can range from 100 CZK ($4.50) to 300 CZK ($13), depending on the event and time of entry. Drinks prices vary, but a typical beer or mixed drink can cost around 70 CZK ($3) or more.

Cross Club - Prague: Cross Club is a unique and eclectic venue that combines a nightclub, music venue, and art space. The club's interior is adorned with industrial and steampunk-inspired decorations, creating an immersive atmosphere.

Cross Club hosts various music events, including electronic, drum and bass, and live performances. Entrance fees are usually around 100 CZK ($4.50) to 150 CZK ($7), and drink prices are similar to other nightlife venues.

Lucerna Music Bar - Prague: Lucerna Music Bar is a popular live music venue and nightclub situated near Wenceslas Square in Prague. It hosts concerts by local and international bands, covering various music genres like rock, pop, and jazz. The venue also features themed parties and DJ nights. Entrance fees depend on the event, ranging from around 100 CZK ($4.50) to 300 CZK ($13). Drink prices are similar to other nightlife establishments in the city.

Music Club Malý Glen - Brno: Music Club Malý Glen is a lively nightlife spot in the city of Brno. It offers a mix of live music performances, DJ sets, and themed parties, catering to different musical tastes. The club has a cozy and intimate atmosphere, attracting both locals and tourists.

Entrance fees vary depending on the event, typically ranging from 50 CZK ($2.25) to 150 CZK ($7). Drink prices are affordable, with beers and mixed drinks starting at around 50 CZK ($2.25).

Mecca Club - Prague: Mecca Club is a popular and upscale nightclub located in Prague's city center. It features multiple dance floors with different music genres, including house, R&B, and hip-hop. The club hosts internationally renowned DJs and attracts a stylish and energetic crowd. Entrance fees can vary significantly depending on the event and time of entry, ranging from around 200 CZK ($9) to 500 CZK ($22). Drink prices tend to be higher in comparison to other nightlife spots in the city.

When visiting nightlife venues in the Czech Republic, keep the following tips in mind:

Dress codes may apply in certain clubs, especially those with a more upscale atmosphere. It's advisable to dress neatly and avoid wearing casual or sporty attire.

Some clubs may require an ID or passport for age verification, as the legal drinking age in the Czech Republic is 18 years old.

Taking public transportation or arranging a designated driver is recommended if you plan to consume alcohol.

These vibrant nightlife spots in the Czech Republic offer a range of musical experiences and energetic atmospheres for visitors to enjoy. Dance the night away, soak up the lively ambiance, and make unforgettable memories during your nighttime adventures in the Czech Republic.

CHAPTER EIGHT: PRACTICAL INFORMATION

Money Matters

Money Matters in the Czech Republic are an essential aspect for tourists to consider during their visit. Here's what you need to know:

- Currency: The Czech koruna (CZK) is the country's official currency. The currency is commonly referred to as "crowns." Notes are available in denominations of 100, 200, 500, 1000, 2000, and 5000 CZK, while coins come in denominations of 1, 2, 5, 10, 20, and 50 CZK.

- Exchanging Currency: Currency exchange offices can be found throughout the Czech Republic, including at airports, train stations, and in major tourist areas. It's advisable to compare exchange rates and fees before making a transaction, as rates may vary between different establishments. Be cautious of exchanging money on the street or in unofficial venues, as they may not provide fair rates. Banks also offer currency exchange services, but they may have limited operating hours.

- ATMs and Credit Cards: ATMs are widely available in cities and towns across the Czech Republic. International debit and credit cards, such as Visa and Mastercard, are generally accepted at most establishments, including hotels, restaurants, and shops. However, it's always a good idea to carry some cash for smaller establishments or in more remote areas where card acceptance may be limited. Be aware that some smaller establishments may only accept cash payments.

- Tipping: Tipping is customary in the Czech Republic, although it's not mandatory. In restaurants, it is common to round up the bill or leave a tip of around 10% of the total amount. If you received excellent service, you can leave a slightly higher tip. Tipping in bars, cafes, and for other services such as taxis is also appreciated, but it is not obligatory. When paying with a card, you can inform the staff the desired tip amount, or you can leave cash on the table for cash transactions.

- Tax Refunds: Tourists from non-European Union countries are eligible for tax refunds on eligible purchases made in the Czech Republic. Shops with "Tax-Free Shopping" or "Premier Tax-Free" signage should be sought out. To claim a tax refund, ensure you request a tax refund form at the time of purchase. At the departure airport, locate the customs desk to get your form stamped before your flight. You can then proceed to the tax refund counter to receive your refund in cash or have it credited back to your credit card.

It's important to note that currency exchange rates, fees, and policies may vary between different establishments and financial institutions. It's advisable to check with your bank or credit card provider regarding any fees associated with international transactions or currency conversions.

By keeping these money matters in mind, you can navigate currency exchanges, transactions, and tipping practices with ease during your visit to the Czech Republic.

Health and Safety

- Travel Insurance: Before visiting the Czech Republic, it's essential to have travel insurance that covers medical expenses and emergency medical evacuation. Ensure that your insurance policy is valid for the entire duration of your trip and provides adequate coverage for your needs.
- Vaccinations: Check with your healthcare provider or travel clinic to verify if any vaccinations are recommended for your visit to the Czech Republic. Routine vaccinations such as measles-mumps-rubella (MMR), diphtheria-tetanus-pertussis, and influenza are generally advised.
- Medications: Make sure you have enough prescription medicine for the length of your

vacation if you take it. Carry your medications in their original packaging, along with the prescriptions, to avoid any issues with customs. Additionally, consider carrying a small first aid kit with basic medical supplies for minor injuries or illnesses.

- Emergency Numbers: Familiarize yourself with the emergency contact numbers in the Czech Republic. The general emergency number is 112, which can be dialed for police, ambulance, or fire services. For non-emergency medical assistance, you can also contact the local healthcare facility or your travel insurance provider.

- COVID-19 Precautions: In light of the ongoing COVID-19 pandemic, it's important to stay informed about the current travel restrictions, entry requirements, and health guidelines implemented by the Czech Republic. Check the official government websites or contact the local embassy or consulate for the most up-to-date information. Follow recommended preventive measures such as wearing masks, practicing good hand hygiene, maintaining physical distancing, and adhering to any specific guidelines or regulations in place.

- General Safety Tips: As with any destination, it's advisable to take general safety precautions. Be aware of your surroundings, especially in crowded tourist areas, and keep an eye on your belongings to prevent theft. Use reputable transportation services and be cautious when using public Wi-Fi networks to protect your personal information.

- Health Facilities: Familiarize yourself with the locations of healthcare facilities, such as hospitals and clinics, in the areas you plan to visit. Carry your travel insurance details, passport, and any relevant medical information with you in case of an emergency.

Remember to consult with your healthcare provider or a travel medicine specialist for personalized advice based on your medical history and specific travel plans. It's also recommended to check the travel advisories issued by your home country's government for any specific health and safety information related to the Czech Republic. By taking necessary precautions and staying informed, you can ensure a safe and healthy trip to the Czech Republic.

Useful Contact Information in the Czech Republic

Emergency Services:

- General Emergency: 112
- Police: 158
- Ambulance: 155
- Fire Department: 150

Consulates and Embassies: It's advisable to have the contact information of your country's embassy or consulate in the Czech Republic in case of emergencies or other assistance.

United States Embassy in Prague:

- Address: Tržiště 15, 118 01 Prague 1
- Phone: +420 257 022 000
- Website: https://cz.usembassy.gov/

United Kingdom Embassy in Prague:

- Address: Thunovská 14, 118 00 Prague 1
- Phone: +420 257 402 111
- Website:
  https://www.gov.uk/world/organisations/briti
  sh-embassy-prague

Canadian Embassy in Prague:

- Address: Velvyslanectví Kanady, Thunovská 14, 118 00 Prague 1
- Phone: +420 272 101 800
- Website:
  https://www.canadainternational.gc.ca/czech
  -republic-tcheque/index.aspx?lang=eng

Czech International Airport:

- Václav Havel Airport Prague:
- Phone: +420 220 111 888

- Website: https://www.prg.aero/en/

Medical Services:

- Emergency Medical Services: 155

Non-emergency Medical Assistance (Prague):

International Clinic Prague:

- Address: Vodičkova 676/31, 110 00 Prague 1
- Phone: +420 222 235 421
- Website: https://www.internationalclinic.cz/

Lost or Stolen Items:

- Contact the local police (emergency: 158) to report lost or stolen items.
- For lost passports or other consular assistance, contact your embassy or consulate in the Czech Republic.

Transportation Services:

Prague Public Transit Company (DPP):

- Phone: +420 296 191 817

- Website: https://www.dpp.cz/en/

Czech Railways (České dráhy):

- Phone: +420 221 111 122
- Website: https://www.cd.cz/en/

Czech Bus Companies:

Student Agency:

- Phone: +420 800 122 333
- Website: https://www.studentagency.eu/

FlixBus:

- Phone: +420 222 222 222
- Website: https://www.flixbus.com/

Remember to save these contact numbers in your phone or have them easily accessible during your stay in the Czech Republic. It's always a good idea to have emergency numbers and important contact information readily available for any unforeseen situations or assistance you may require during your trip.

Final Tips and Recommendations for Your Trip to the Czech Republic:

Learn Some Basic Czech Phrases: While many people in tourist areas speak English, learning a few basic Czech phrases can go a long way in showing respect and making connections with locals. Simple greetings like "Dobrý den" (Good day) and "Děkuji" (Thank you) can make a positive impression.

Stay Hydrated: Carry a water bottle with you, especially during the summer months, as staying hydrated is important while exploring the Czech Republic. Tap water is generally safe to drink, so refilling your bottle from public water fountains or restaurants can help you save money and reduce plastic waste.

Respect Local Customs and Etiquette: Familiarize yourself with Czech customs and etiquette to ensure a smooth and respectful interaction with locals. For example, it's customary to greet people with a handshake, remove your shoes when entering someone's home, and avoid discussing sensitive topics like politics or religion unless invited to do so.

Be Mindful of Scams and Pickpocketing: Like any tourist destination, be cautious of scams and pickpocketing. Keep a watch on your possessions, particularly in busy places and on public transit. Avoid exchanging money on the street and use reputable currency exchange offices or banks.

Explore Beyond Prague: While Prague is undoubtedly captivating, consider venturing outside the capital to discover the country's diverse regions. Places like Český Krumlov, Karlovy Vary, Brno, and the Bohemian and Moravian countryside offer their own unique charms and attractions.

Enjoy Czech Cuisine and Beer: Indulge in Czech cuisine and savor the local flavors. Don't miss the opportunity to try traditional dishes like goulash, svíčková, and trdelník. And of course, sample the world-renowned Czech beer, as the country has a rich brewing tradition.

Embrace the Rich History and Culture: The Czech Republic has a fascinating history and a vibrant cultural scene. Take time to explore historical sites, visit museums, and attend cultural events or concerts to fully immerse yourself in the country's heritage.

Farewell to Czech: As your trip to the Czech Republic comes to an end, we hope you have had a wonderful experience exploring this beautiful country. May the memories you've created stay with you as you bid farewell to the Czech Republic. Safe travels and we hope to welcome you back again in the future! Na shledanou!

Printed in Great Britain
by Amazon